FloridaOneTankTrips.com

FLORIDA ONE TANK TRIPS
VOLUME 2

Fifty Nifty Places You Can Visit On One Tank Of Gas

First Edition 2018

Mike Miller

INTRODUCTION

This book is part of a series that began with Florida One Tank Trips Volume I. Like the first book, Volume II features 50 attractions – each one different than those featured in Volume 1.

As this book is published in 2018, many families cannot afford the steep admission fees for a day or two at the major theme parks such as Walt Disney World, Universal Studios Florida, and SeaWorld. A family of four can typically find it costs them more than $400 just to get in and a huge amount on top of that for food and drink and extra attractions once they are inside.

Florida One Tank Trips Volume 2 fills the need for a handy directory to more affordable attractions, all within a one tank drive of one of six major Florida cities: Jacksonville, Miami, Orlando, Pensacola, Tallahassee and Tampa.

Each attraction in the book is described and includes information on admission fees, operating hours, and contact information including address, telephone number and website.

Volume 2 features 50 of these attractions. Future volumes in this series will cover even more of them, 50 at a time.

You will find yourself having a lot of fun and saving a lot of money.

AUTHOR

Mike Miller has lived in Florida since 1960. He graduated from the University of Florida with a degree in civil engineering and has lived and worked in most areas of Florida. His projects include Walt Disney World, EPCOT, Universal Studios and hundreds of commercial, municipal and residential developments all over the state.

During that time, Mike developed an understanding and love of Old Florida that is reflected in the pages of his website, **Florida-Backroads-Travel.com** and in several other books he has written on Florida subjects.

If you have enjoyed this book and purchased it on **Amazon**, Mike would appreciate it if you would take a couple of minutes to post a short review at Amazon. Thoughtful reviews help other customers make better buying choices. He reads all of his reviews personally, and each one helps him write better books in the future. Thanks for your support!

FLORIDA'S 8 GEOGRAPHICAL REGIONS

TABLE OF CONTENTS

ORLANDO AND CENTRAL FLORIDA

TAMPA AND WEST FLORIDA

PENSACOLA AND NORTHWEST FLORIDA

TALLHASSEE AND NORTH CENTRAL FLORIDA

JACKSONVILLE AND NORTHEAST FLORIDA

MIAMI AND SOUTHEAST FLORIDA

FRANK LLOYD WRIGHT
CHILD OF THE SUN

Florida Southern College in Lakeland is home to several buildings designed by Frank Lloyd Wright from 1941 to 1958. This collection is named Child of the Sun. All of the structures are on the National Register of Historic Places, and are working buildings used by students and faculty.

The Child of the Sun Visitor Center has photographs, furniture and working drawings related to Wright's work on the campus. The Center also has a gift shop, and seasonal tours are offered of the Wright designed buildings by appointment only.

You can also tour the campus on your own, creating your own self guided tour. Maps are available in the tourism center.

BASIC INFORMATION

Florida Southern College
111 Lake Hollingsworth Drive
Lakeland, Florida 33801
863-680-4597
fllw@flsouthern.edu

Admission Fees: The Basic Tour is $20/person, a longer in-depth tour is $35/person.

Hours: Basic Tours are daily at 10am. Self guided tours are permitted between 930am to 430pm

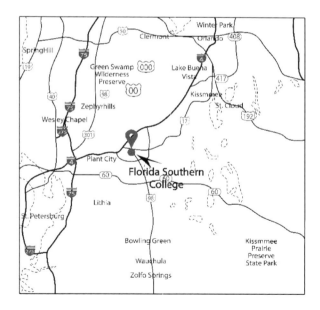

HONEST JOHN'S FISH CAMP

Honest John's is at the end of a dirt road on the Indian River Lagoon 5 miles north of Sebastian Inlet. It is the homestead of Robert T. Smith and his family. It dates back to 1887.

This fish camp has no lodging and no restaurant. It does have Old Florida ambiance and a feeling of history. The old cracker house that Robert Smith built in 1889 is still on the property.

Hens, roosters, pigs, ducks and a dog have free range over the property. You can go on eco-tours, look at birds, dolphins, and manatees. You can also go fishing or take sailboard lessons.

The owners are the Arthur family, direct descendants of Robert T. Smith and his son Honest John. Barbara Arthur is a local historian and a world champion fisherwoman.

BASIC INFORMATION

750 Old Florida Trail
Melbourne Beach, Florida 32951
Tel: 321-727-2923
honestjohnsfishcamp.com

Admission Fees: Free

Hours: Open 6 am to 6 pm every day but Tuesday.

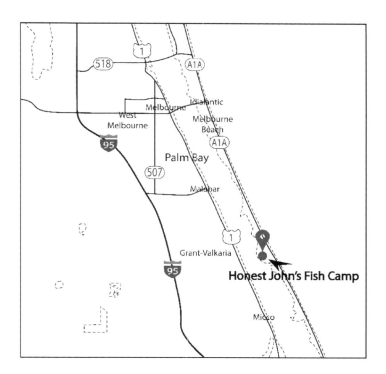

LAKE PLACID MURALS

Lake Placid is a small town of about 2200 people south of Sebring on U.S. Highway 27. It proudly wears two titles: "The Caladium Capital of the World" and the "Town of Murals". The flowers are celebrated each year in a festival. Almost all of the world's caladium bulbs come from the Lake Placid area.

The other title comes from the fact that this small village has more than 40 murals painted on various buildings throughout the downtown section. Some of the murals portray events from the illustrious history of Lake Placid.

The town was originally named Lake Stearns. Dr. Melvil Dewey, inventor of the Dewey Decimal System, had founded the Lake Placid Club in New York and lobbied to have the town renamed Lake Placid.

BASIC INFORMATION

Lake Placid Chamber of Commerce
18 North Oak Avenue
Lake Placid, Florida 33852
863-465-4331
lpfla.com

Admission Fees: Admission to the town is free. The annual Caladium Festival charges extra.

Hours: The town is open all the time.

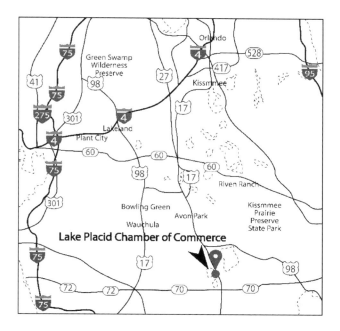

MOUNT DORA SEGWAY

Mount Dora is a scenic town of about 12,000 people in the hilly lake country about 28 miles northwest of downtown Orlando. It reminds many people of a New England town with its oak canopied streets and historic homes.

The guided Segway tours last about one hour and take you through several interesting areas of town. Tours are limited to riders 14 years old or more, between 100 and 260 pounds, and in good enough condition to step on and off the Segway. Helmets are provided to all riders.

One of the tours takes you through the Mount Dora historic district, including the boardwalk on Lake Dora and the lighthouse. A secondary tour takes you to Lake Gertrude and up Dogwood Mountain, a naturally scenic part of town.

BASIC INFORMATION

430 N. Alexander Street
Mount Dora, Florida 32757
352-460-2039
centralfloridaguides.com

Admission Fees: Tours are by reservation only and cost $49 each.

Hours: Daily Monday through Sunday: 930am, 1130am, 130pm

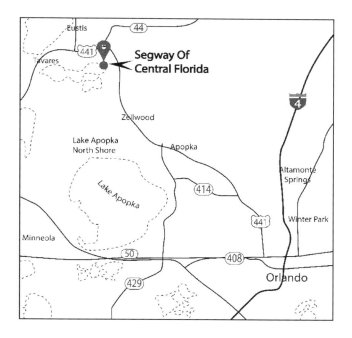

OLD TOWN IN KISSIMMEE

Old Town is a shopping center where you park your car and walk through what appears to be an Old Florida town. It is located on US-192 in Kissimmee a few miles west of Walt Disney World. The center is on 18 acres and the tree lined streets paved with brick give you a hometown feeling.

The architecture is reminiscent of a classic old Florida town. The storefronts capture the architecture f and earlier time in Florida. The district has 70 shops, various restaurants and bars, rides, and attractions for the entire family.

Old Town hosts many weekly events such as a car show and cruise in every Saturday that attracts hundreds of classic cars. There is a large parking lot, and parking is free.

BASIC INFORMATION

5770 West Irlo Bronson Highway
Kissimmee, Florida 34746
407-396-4888
myoldtownusa.cor

Admission Fees: Free. Rides and restaurants have fees.

Hours: Open Daily 10am to 11pm, Restaurants 10am to 10pm

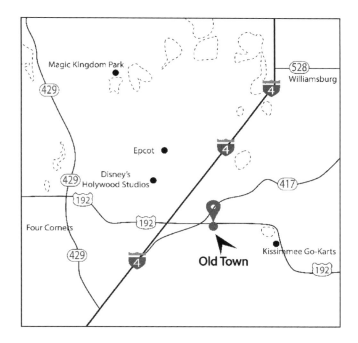

ORANGE COUNTY
REGIONAL HISTORY CENTER

This history center is an affiliate of the Smithsonian Institution and is located in a historic courthouse. It contains the collection of the Historical Society of Central Florida, a research library, a gift shop, and Heritage Square Park.

The center is located in downtown Orlando and showcases 12,000 years of Central Florida history. Exhibits include African American history, aviation, cattle and citrus, tourism, the Spanish era, Native Americans, and the natural environment.

There is even a Florida pioneer cabin showing how early settlers lived in Central Florida. The center also touches on the history of Central Florida's many theme parks.

BASIC INFORMATION

65 E. Central Boulevard
Orlando, Florida 32801
407-836-8500
thehistorycenter.org

Admission Fees: Adults $8, Children (5-12) $6, Florida
Educators Free, Seniors $7 plus other discounts

Hours: Monday-Saturday 10am to 5pm;   Sunday Noon to 5pm

ORLANDO SIGNIFICANT TREE TOUR

The City of Orlando values its many ancient trees and has established a "Significant Tree Program" that includes majestic trees near downtown Orlando. There are 7 locations that these trees call home and all are maintained and protected by the City of Orlando.

The locations are 1. Langford Park; 2. Dickson Azalea Park; 3. Constitution Green Park; 4. Lake Eola Park; 5. Big Tree Park; 6. Harry P. Leu Gardens, and 7. Loch Haven Park. The oldest tree in Orlando is located in Big Tree Park and is reported to be 350 to 400 years old.

You can take a self guided tour in your own car and enjoy all of these trees except the one in Leu Gardens (an admission fee is charged there). A tree tour map is available on the City of Orlando website.

BASIC INFORMATION

http://www.cityoforlando.net/blog/orlando-home-to-numerous-significant-trees/

Admission Fees: Free except for Harry P. Leu Gardens

Hours: Best to take the tour during off peak traffic hours.

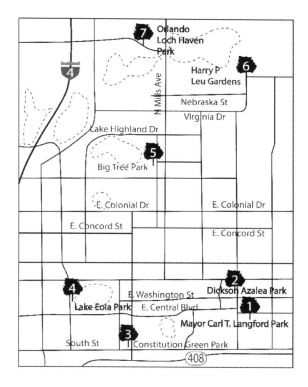

RON JON SURF SHOP

Ron Jon Surf Shop started in 1959 as a small surf board and clothing shop in New Jersey. It opened its Cocoa Beach store a few years later and has expanded to more than a dozen other locations across the country.

The Cocoa Beach   store is the flagship of the entire company and is a treat to visit with every imaginable kind of beach clothing and accessories. Needless to say, they also sell a huge variety of surf boards.

You are free to wander around the store and look at whatever you want. Ron Jon's has become so popular that they now offer group tours for school groups or senior citizen clubs. Parking is available on the property in two different lots: one if you expect to visit for less than 90 minutes, the other for longer visits.

BASIC INFORMATION

4151 North Atlantic Avenue (State Rd A1A)
Cocoa Beach, Florida 32931
321-799-8888
ronjonsurfshop.com

Admission Fees: Free

Hours: Open 7 days/week, 24 hours/day.

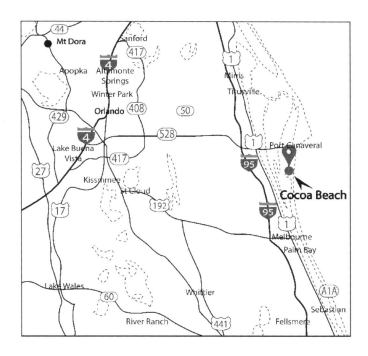

SEA TURTLES NESTING ON BEACH

Florida has an abundant supply of beautiful sand beaches, and every year from May to October is sea turtle nesting season. The turtles crawl up the beach to the dune line, dig holes in the sand, and lay their eggs. Some experts say that sea turtles make 40,000 to 84,000 nests each year on Florida beaches.

A favorite place to observe this nesting activity is on Florida's east coast. The Sea Turtle Preservation Society is located near the center of this stretch in Indialantic near Melbourne Beach. During nesting season all oceanfront homes and motels are required to draw their drapes or turn off their lights so as not to confuse the mother turtles as they crawl up from the ocean.

Sea turtles and their nests are strictly protected. It is illegal to disturb a mother laying her eggs or the nest after she's gone. Some motels and organizations along the beach can tell you the proper way and place to enjoy this natural spectacle.

BASIC INFORMATION

Sea Turtle Preservation Society
111 South Miramar Avenue
Indialantic, Florida 32903
321-676-1701

Admission Fees: Free

Hours: Best time to view is after sunset or before sunrise.

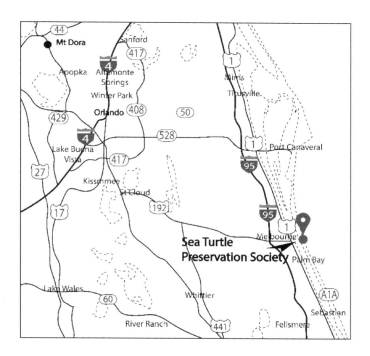

SPOOK HILL

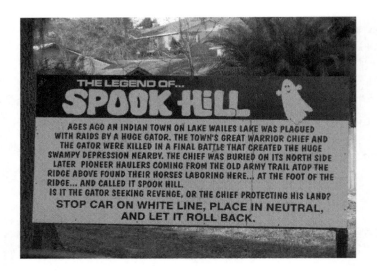

Spook Hill is an optical illusion attraction that has been entertaining people for a very long time. The illusion is that when you park your car at the bottom of the hill and put it in neutral, it appears to be coasting slowly up the hill, defying gravity.

A white line has been painted on the street so you know where to park your car. If all goes as expected, your car will start its self powered trip up the hill.

Although there are several folk legends about why this happens, the truth is that the lay of the land and growth pattern of the trees makes it look like up is down and vice versa. It doesn't matter to you because you still experience that mystical feeling of beating gravity at its own game.

BASIC INFORMATION

Lake Wales, Florida 33853 (see map); adjacent to Spook Hill Elementary School

Admission Fees: Free

Hours: 7 days/week, 24 hours/day

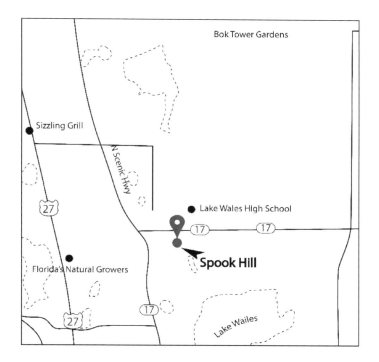

WHISPERING OAKS WINERY

Whispering Oaks is all about blueberries. It is located on a large blueberry farm in Oxford, Florida near The Villages. The farm has 40,000 blueberry bushes so it is only natural that the winery's specialty is blueberry wine.

Part of the fun of visiting this winery is going on a tour of the facility conducted by the owner, Johannes Vanderwey. He hired an international wine expert to help him create his unique selection of wines.

The visitors center has a friendly little bar that serves blueberry wine and has a nice ambiance to it. Johannes points out that there are two pounds of blueberries in every bottle of wine.

The shaded deck at the visitor center has a nice pond with a waterfall, and entertainment is provided on weekends.

BASIC INFORMATION

10934 County Road 475
Oxford, Florida 34484
352-748-0449
winesofflorida.com

Admission Fees: Free

Hours: Monday-Thursday: 11am to 7pm.
Friday, Saturday and Sunday: 11am to 9pm

C'D'ZAN RINGLING SARASOTA HOME

John Ringling made his fortune in the circus business. He and his brothers operated the circus known as "The Greatest Show on Earth". Ca'd'Zan is a mansion constructed in the Venetian Gothic Style. The name in English means "House of John".

In addition to the mansion, the Ringling complex includes the Museum of Art and the Circus Museum. A museum ticket gets you into both museums, but not into the mansion itself. You can buy a special ticket that includes admission to the museums and a tour of Ca'd'Zan led by a docent.

There are so many tour and admission options that it is highly recommended you go to the website before visiting so you can make the right decision about what you want to see and what time you want to see it.

BASIC INFORMATION

5401 Bay Shore Road
Sarasota, Florida 34243
941-359-57000
www.ringling.org

Admission Fees: Varies from $15 up depending on option chosen. See website for detailed information.

Hours: Daily, 10am to 500pm. Thursdays until 8pm.

CRYSTAL RIVER MANATEE SWIM

Crystal River is a small town 70 miles north of Tampa where the West Indian Manatee like to congregate in the waters that are crystal clear and a year round comfortable temperature of 72 degrees F. Manatees cannot survive in water that is colder than 60 degrees, so this location is perfect for them.

There are numerous businesses in Crystal River that will take you on snorkeling expeditions so you can visit with what is estimated to be as many as 400 of the giant gentle creatures who come here   You can also rent kayaks or canoes and create you own do-it-yourself tour or go on a guided one.

The best time to visit is November through March when you can swim with the manatees or just observe them from a boat or a dock in Kings Bay. These gentle animals can grow to be 12 or 13 feet long and weigh more than 3000 pounds.

BASIC INFORMATION

American Pro Diving Center
821 US Highway 19
Crystal River, FL 34429
352-563-0041
americanprodiving.com

Admission Fees: Tours from $58 per person and up.

Hours: Varies, sometimes starting as early as 630 am

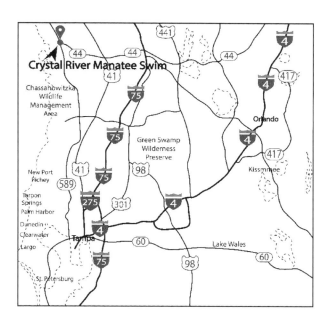

FORT DESOTO PARK

Fort De Soto Park is the largest park in the Pinellas County park system with 1,136 acres comprised of five interconnected islands. The park is south of St. Petersburg Beach and Tierra Verde and is reached from the mainland by County Road 679.

The islands that make up the park are among the most natural environment in Florida. There are mangroves, wetlands, beach plants, palm hammocks, hardwoods and numerous native plants of all kinds. It is reported that the islands are home to more than 328 species of birds.

The park has more than 7 miles of waterfront, and 3 of those miles are some of the most beautiful beaches in the United States. Things to do include visiting the historic fort, camping, swimming, nature trail hiking, launching your own boat, renting kayaks and bikes, and fishing from a park pier.

BASIC INFORMATION

3500 Pinellas Bayway South
Tierra Verde, Florida 33715
727-582-2267
www.pinellascounty.org/park/05_ft_desoto.htm

Admission Fees: Daily parking fee $5. Extra for camping, boat launching, bike and kayak rentals, etc.

Hours: County parks are open 7 days/week from 7am to dusk. Open 365 days/year including Thanksgiving and Christmas

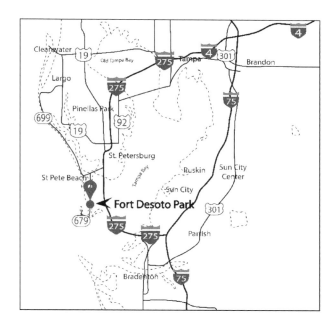

LOWRY PARK ZOO

Tampa's Lowry Park Zoo is one of the most popular zoos in Florida, with over 1 million annual visitors. The zoo occupies 56 acres of naturalistic animal exhibits in a tropical garden setting and has many up-close animal encounters that kids and adults both enjoy.

The zoo pays special attention to endangered species from world climates similar to that of the Tampa Bay area. There are park zones devoted to Asia, Africa, Australia and Florida. More than 1,300 separate animals have their permanent homes in the zoo.

Another interesting feature of this zoo is their Manatee Critical Care Center, the only one of its kind in Florida. Zoo guests can have the experience of watching through windows while the zoo staff treat injured and orphaned manatees.

BASIC INFORMATION

1101 West Sligh Avenue
Tampa, Florida 33604
813-935-8552
www.lowryparkzoo.org

Admission Fees: Adults, $32.95, Children (3-11), $24,95. See
the website for specials and various discounts

Hours: Open 7 days/week from 930am to 500pm except
Thanksgiving and Christmas.

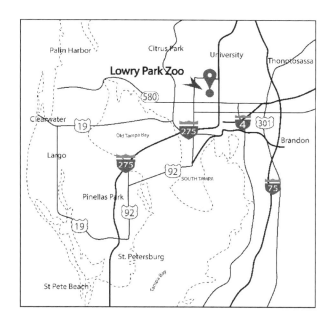

MOTE MARINE LABORATORY
& AQUARIUM

Mote is an independent research institution with a staff of marine scientists dedicated to the belief that research and education is the key to the conservation and sustainable use of our oceans. The institution originally specialized in the study of sharks, but in recent years their scope has greatly increased.

They not only conduct studies of human cancer using marine models, they also research the effects of toxins on humans and fisheries. They study the population dynamics of manatees, dolphins, sea turtles, sharks, and coral reefs.

Visitors are welcome to enjoy the working aquarium which has a variety of marine animals and fish along with two touch tanks and a 135,000 gallon shark habitat, and more than 100 species.

BASIC INFORMATION

1600 Ken Thompson Parkway
Sarasota, Florida 34236
941-388-4441
https://mote.org/aquarium

Admission Fees: Adults $22, Youth (3-12) $16, Children free.

Hours: Open 7 days/week, 365 days/year, 1000am to 500pm

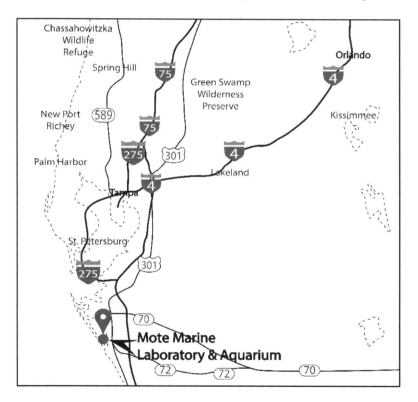

RIVER SAFARIS

River Safaris is located in Old Homosassa on a waterway that leads to the Homosassa River and passes Monkey Island. You park your car at the site and have a wide variety of things you can enjoy. They have rental boats, a gift shop and art gallery, and three alligators who live in a pen on the site.

You can spend a day in Homosassa doing a variety of things and base your adventures from here. They have airboat tours, boat rentals, pontoon boat tours, manatee tours, group tours, scalloping and fishing adventures, and more.

They have such a large variety of adventures available it is advisable to visit their website to get an idea. In addition to the various tours and manatee swims, you can even go on a two hour twilight dolphin watching and tiki bar tour.

BASIC INFORMATION

10823 West Yulee Drive
Homosassa, Florida 34448
352-628-5222
riversafaris.com

Admission Fees: Each tour has its own fee. Check website for specific details

Hours: Hours vary depending on the tour or adventure. Check website for specific details

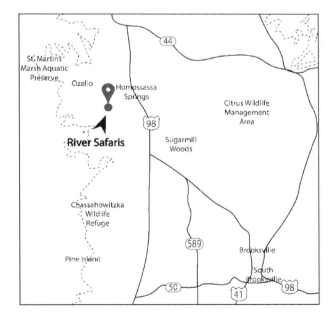

SUNKEN GARDENS

Sunken Gardens is a century old botanical garden in the middle of busy urban St. Petersburg. You will enjoy winding paths surrounded by exotic plants from all regions of the world. You can also sign up for garden tours, horticultural programs, special events and field trips.

Your tour will take you past cascading waterfalls, demonstration gardens, and more than 50,000 tropical plants and flowers. Some recent special events included Frogs and Toads, Colorful Caladiums, and Easy Care Natives and Wildflowers.

When you check into the gardens you will be provided a map that gives you details on the various plants. Parking is free at Sunken Gardens

BASIC INFORMATION

1825 4th Street North
St. Petersburg, Florida 33704
727-551-3102
www.stpete.org/attractions/sunken_gardens/index.php

Admission Fees: $10 Adults, $8 Seniors, $4 Children

Hours: Mon-Sat, 1000am to 430pm. Sunday, Noon to 430pm
Closed Thanksgiving and Christmas

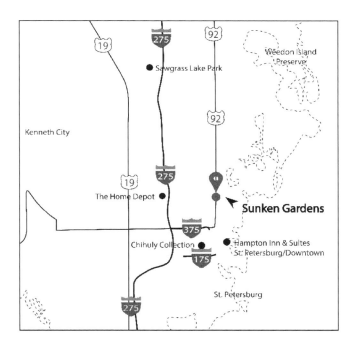

WITHLACOOCHEE STATE TRAIL

The Withlacoochee State Trail is a 46 mile long path on abandoned railroad tracks that follows a route roughly parallel to the nearby Withlacoochee River. The path is now paved and is a great location to hike, bike (no motors), and skate. It's mostly flat so even geezers and out of shape people can enjoy it.

You can start the path at either end (north or south) or at one of the towns or villages along the route. The northern end is at the town of Dunnellon and the southern end is near a tiny old railroad town named Trilby.

There are stores in Dunnellon, Inverness, and Floral City where you can rent a bike if you don't have your own. There are also restroom facilities and restaurants located conveniently near the path at several locations.

BASIC INFORMATION

Admission Fees: Free

Hours: Every day, sunrise to sunset

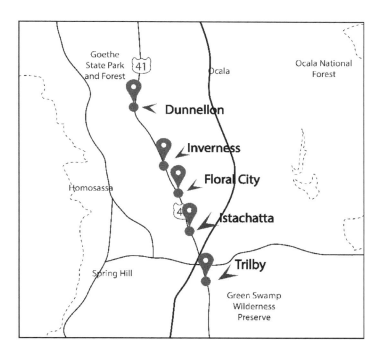

AIR FORCE ARMAMENT MUSEUM

The museum showcases the armament of aviation warfare from World War One all the way through to today's super sophisticated high technology planes, guns, and bombs. They have a large collection of weapons and cockpit simulators that will keep an aviation buff busy for hours.

As you drive onto the museum property you will see many aircraft on display, including the SR-71 Blackbird, the fastest plane ever built. There are other planes from World War Two, the Korean War, Vietnam, and Gulf War eras.

There are four more aircraft inside of the museum building itself, as well as a huge variety of bombs, missiles and rockets. Displays include the AMRAAM and GBU bunker buster.

BASIC INFORMATION

100 Museum Drive
Eglin Air Force, Florida 32542
850-882-4062
www.afarmamentmuseum.com

Admission Fees: Free

Hours: Monday-Saturday, 930am to 430pm. Closed on Federal
Holidays. Outdoor park with 25 planes open in daytime.

DESTIN SAND CASTLE LESSONS

Most people have tried to build a sand castle at least once in their lives. Destin Sand Castle Lessons takes this skill to a whole new level. The beautiful sand beaches around Destin have attracted several businesses that will teach you how to build your ultimate sand castle.

You can either have a sand sculpture expert build one for you or learn how to build one yourself. The operation is all along the Gulf Coast from Destin east along Highway 30A to Seaside and Inlet Beach. The website will give you further details.

If you take a lesson, it usually last about two hours to show you the right tools, the proper sand-water blend, and help along the way as you try your hand at this fun adventure. When the lesson is complete you will have your very own 3.5 foot tall sculpture ready for photographs of the entire family.

BASIC INFORMATION

Beach Sand Sculptures, LLC
P.O. Box 1988
Santa Rosa Beach, Florida 32459
beachsandsculptures.com

Admission Fees: Various charges depending on the lesson or sculpture chosen. The larger your group, the less the cost per person. Check website for details of adventures and prices.

Hours: Depends on appointment reservations.

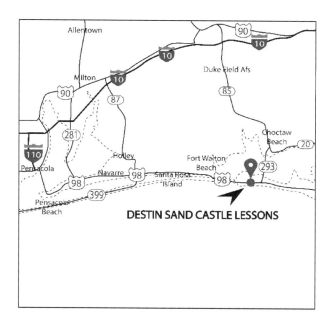

DESTIN SAND CASTLE LESSONS

FLORIDA CAVERNS STATE PARK

This state park has dry (air filled) caves and is the only Florida park to offer cave tours to the public. The Florida Caverns have some impressive formations of stalactites, stalagmites, soda straws, flowstones, and draperies. All of these features are natural limestone formations.

The park is also home to the Chipola River and Blue Spring with abundant opportunities for fishing, canoeing, kayaking, camping, and picnicking. There is even a nine hole golf course available to park visitors.

Guided cave tours are offered all year long except Thanksgiving and Christmas. The average tour takes 45 minutes and is considered moderately strenuous.

BASIC INFORMATION

3345 Caverns Road
Marianna, Florida 32446
850-482-1228
www.floridastateparks.org/park/Florida-Caverns

Admission Fees: $5.00 per vehicle (2-8 people). Cave tours are $8.00 per person age 13 older, $5.00 per child.

Hours: 800am to sunset, 365 days a year. Cave tours are not available on Thanksgiving and Christmas Day.

GULFARIUM MARINE ADVENTURE PARK

The mission of Gulfarium is to educate, entertain, and inspire its guests to respect and preserve wildlife by providing unique and memorable experiences that will help people of all ages connect with marine life.

There are a large number of animal encounters here, including those with dolphins, stingrays, gators, reptiles turtles, penguins, seals, sea lions, and birds. The even have a feature called Breakfast with the Dolphins.

The Gulfarium team of specialists is continually on hand to help and inform you through the various animal encounter adventures. Most of the encounters require an advance reservation.

BASIC INFORMATION

1010 Miracle Strip Parkway SE
Fort Walton Beach, Florida 32548
850-243-9046
www.gulfarium.com

Admission Fees: $21.95 Adults, $13.95 Children.

Hours: Daily, 900am to 530pm except Christmas and
Thanksgiving. Admission closes at 430pm

JOHN GORRIE STATE MUSEUM

It's hard to imagine living in hot humid Florida without air conditioning, but there was a time when that was the way of life. This museum celebrates the life of Dr. John Gorrie, who is widely accepted as the inventor of modern air conditioning.

Dr. Gorrie was trying to cool the rooms of his yellow fever patients in the 1800s and invented a machine to make ice. He received a U.S. Patent for mechanical refrigeration in 1851. A replica of his ice making machine is on display at the museum, and other exhibits showing the colorful history of Apalachicola.

A Florida State Park Ranger will help you understand the history and contributions of Dr. Gorrie, and also fill you in on local history. Including its seafood industry and other natural resources.

BASIC INFORMATION

46 6th Street
Apalachicola, Florida 32320
850-653-9347
www.floridastateparks.org/park-history/john-gorrie-museum

Admission Fees: $2.00 per person, children under 5 are free

Hours: Thursday-Monday, 900am to 500pm except
Thanksgiving, Christmas, and New Years Day.

PENSACOLA HISTORIC VILLAGE

Historic Pensacola is a neighborhood of 28 historic buildings and museums. The village is managed by the University of West Florida Historic Trust and is located in the historic district of downtown Pensacola. The entire historic district features charming homes, museums, art galleries, restaurants, and shops. Pensacola's history goes back more than 450 years.

Among the properties you will see are the T.T. Wentworth, Jr. Museum; Pensacola Children's Museum; Museum of Commerce; Museum of Industry; Old Christ Church; Tivoli High House, Dorr House; Julee Cottage, Fountain Park; and Colonial Archaeological Trail.

Both guided and self guided tours are available and there is a wide variety of them available to the visitor.

BASIC INFORMATION

120 Church Street
Pensacola, Florida 32502
850-595-5985
www.historicpensacola.org

Admission Fees: Adults $8.00, Child (3-14) $4.00

Hours: Tuesday-Saturday, 100am to 400pm.

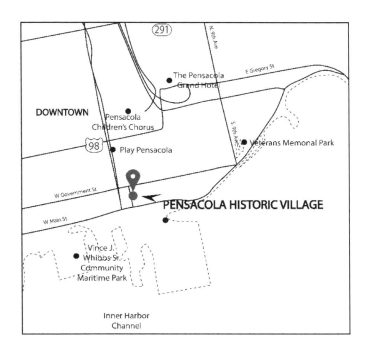

SAM'S FUN CITY

Sam's Fun City is an amusement and water park located in Pensacola. It features over 20 rides and other attractions that kids and adults alike will enjoy. Sam's also has a huge arcade loaded with 75 games. They even have a laser tag arena.

Among the things you can enjoy at Sam's are go carts, bumper boats, miniature golf, and water slides. Food is available at Bullwinkle's Family Food 'n Fun which features pizzas, hot dogs, hamburgers, corn dogs, salads, and deli sandwiches.

Sam's Surf City is adjacent to Sam's fun city and has a separate admission fee. Sam's has a fireworks show every Friday at 900pm and always has a deal of the day where you can, for example, have unlimited use of go carts and laser tag all day long. Most day visitors spend 3.5 hours at Sam's Fun City.

BASIC INFORMATION

6709 Pensacola Boulevard
Pensacola, Florida 32505
850-505-0800
samsfuncity.com

Admission Fees: $26.99 to $37.99 depending on rides and attractions selected. See website for details.

Hours: Sunday through Thursday, 1100am to 900pm. Friday and Saturday 1100am to 1000pm.

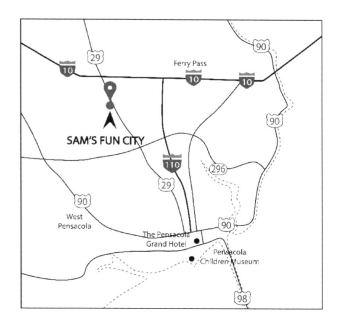

ZOO WORLD

The full name of this attraction is ZooWorld Zoological and Botanical Conservatory. The zoo specializes on conservation as has over 260 animals with numerous exhibits, programs, and performances in a tropical setting.

This is an interactive attraction where you can do various thing with the animals. Examples include Sloth Encounter, Giraffe Feeding Tower, Lemur Encounter, Hold and Alligator, Budgie Bush-Walk Aviary, and more. These encounters usually include your holding and petting the animal.

Most of the encounters cost you extra in addition to the general admission fee. A typical charge for these encounters is $35 per person. There are also various dispensers around the zoo where you can pay extra to buy food to feed the animals. An affordable day might be to limit the encounters to the children in your group.

BASIC INFORMATION

9008 Front Beach Road
Panama City Beach, FL 32407
850-230-1243
zooworldpcb.com

Admission Fees: Adults $16.59, Children (2-12) $12.95

Hours: Open daily from 930am to 500pm

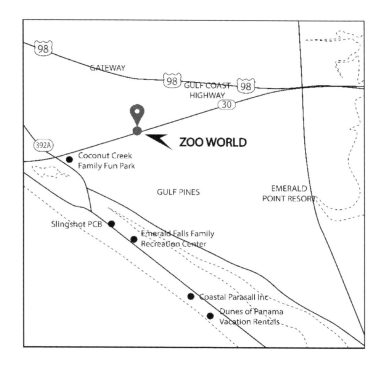

BOB'S RIVER PLACE

An elderly gentleman named Bob Hawkins owns this popular tourist attraction on the Suwannee River near Branford. He originally bought 40 acres with a half mile of riverfront in the early 1970s and built his house on a bluff overlooking the river.

The venture started with a tree house and swing that Bob built for his children. He wanted the kids to experience the fun of a good old fashioned swimming hole like he had enjoyed as a kid. Over the years he and friends added water slides, rope swings, docks, tree ladders so you can jump into the river from a tree, a waterwheel, and picnic shelters.

Bob Hawkins is now in his eighties but is usually on site during operating hours. It's pretty obvious he does not do this for the money. He enjoys people and this is his way of meeting them.

BASIC INFORMATION

2878 County Road 340
Branford, Florida 32008
352-542-7363
bobsriverplace.com

Admission Fees: Parking is the only fee. $25/car (3 people or less), $35/car (4 to 6 people), everything else is free

Hours: Open 7 days/week from 1100am to 600pm

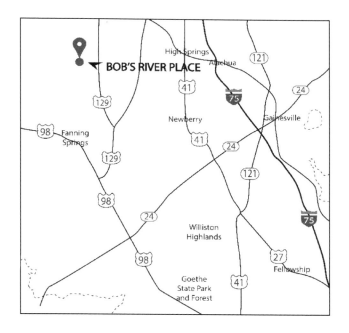

CROSS CREEK

Cross Creek was the home of Marjorie Kinnan Rawlings, who chronicled Florida Cracker and Florida Black life in her stories and books, among them "The Yearling", "South Moon Under," and "Cross Creek." Her home has been preserved much as it was when she lived her and is open part of the year for tours.

In addition to preserving the home that Marjorie moved into in 1928, the grounds also include ornamental plants, a kitchen garden, and citrus grove, and a tenant house. The Yearling is a local restaurant that serves good Florida Cracker food.

Marjorie's love for Cross Creek is summed up in her own words: "Cross Creek belongs to the wind and the rain, to the sun and the seasons, to the cosmic secrecy of seed, and beyond all, to time."

BASIC INFORMATION

18700 County Road 325
Hawthorne, Florida 32640
352-466-3672
www.floridastateparks.org/park/Marjorie-Kinnan-Rawlings

Admission Fees: $3 per group in one vehicle. Honor box used so correct change is required. Guided tours are extra.

Hours: Open daily from 900am to 500pm. Guided tours from October through July on hourly basis from 1000am to 400pm.

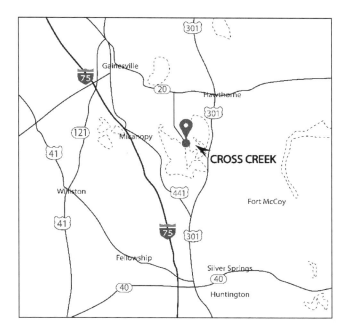

CEDAR KEY

Cedar Key is a small fishing and tourist town at the end of State Road 24 on the Gulf of Mexico. About 700 people call this little village their permanent home. State Road 24 runs from Gainesville to Cedar Key, a straight line trip of about 60 miles.

The village has several good seafood restaurants, and it's fun to just drive around and look at the weathered old houses and get a feel for what genuine Old Florida was all about.

Depending on when you visit, you might be able to enjoy on of the festivals that take place every year in Cedar Key. The Annual Fine Arts Festival is held on the last weekend of March, and the Cedar Key Seafood Festival is held on the third weekend in October.

BASIC INFORMATION

State Road 24 runs across Florida through Gainesville and terminates in Cedar Key. It follows the route of Florida's first trans-state railroad. Just stay on this highway until you reach the Gulf of Mexico

Admission Fees: Free

Hours: 24 hours/day

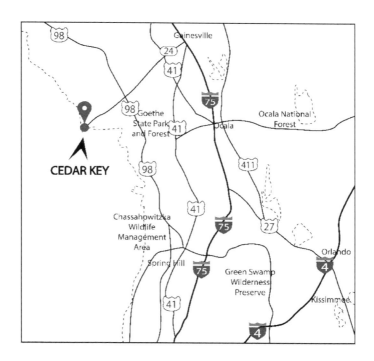

DEVIL'S MILLHOPPER

A visit to the Devil's Millhopper State Geological State Park is a right of passage for University of Florida students. Non-Gators will also get a great kick out of visiting this unusual attraction.

The Devil's Millhopper is a 120 foot deep sinkhole about 500 feet in diameter whose bottom is a tropical rain forest. As you walk down the winding wooden stairway to the bottom, you will see small streams of water - miniature waterfalls - trickling down the steep sides.

This natural bowl is filled with tropical vegetation and stays cool even on the hottest summer days. You can bring you own food and enjoy a picnic and learn about this unique place through interpretative displays located throughout the park.

Devil's Millhopper has been designated a National Natural Landmark.

BASIC INFORMATION

4732 Millhopper Road
Gainesville, Florida 32653
352-955-2008
https://www.floridastateparks.org/park/Devils-Millhopper

Admission Fees: $4.00/vehicle up to 8 passengers

Hours: 9:00 am to 5:00 pm Wednesday through Sunday.
Closed on Monday and Tuesday.

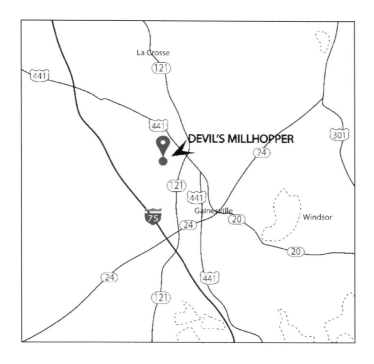

DON GARLIT'S MUSEUM OF DRAG RACING

Don Garlit's is well known as a race car driver and automotive engineer. He is considered the father of drag racing. His nickname is "Big Daddy", and he has a world-wide following, and a member of several Halls of Fame.

His museum in Ocala opened in 1976 and chronicles the history of the sport of drag racing. The museum has almost 300 cars on display, including 90 racing cars and 50 antique cars.

The museum is also home to the International Drag Racing Hall of Fame. One of the special admission features is that for an additional cost, you can get a private tour conducted by "Big Daddy" himself that will show you private garage areas not open to the general public.

BASIC INFORMATION

13700 SW 16th Avenue
Ocala, Florida 34473
352-245-8661
http://garlits.com/

Admission Fees: $20 adults, $15 seniors, Teenagers $15, Children $10 (ages 5-12)

Hours: 9:00 am to 5:00 pm daily. Closed Thanksgiving and Christmas.

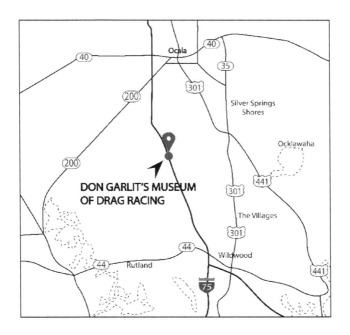

MUSEUM OF FLORIDA HISTORY

The Museum of Florida History in Tallahassee is a giant collection of Florida history artifacts and information that the entire family will enjoy. The museum focuses on past and present cultures in the State of Florida.

It is the official State of Florida history museum, and has a lot of information on Florida's development and the heritage and history of the state.

The museum has hundreds of exhibits, educational programs, research projects, and collections. Among the permanent exhibits is Florida in the Civil War, World War II, and La Florida – the era between 1513 and 1821. You will learn about Florida during its period of being Spanish, British, Confederate, and American.

BASIC INFORMATION

500 S. Bronough
Tallahassee, Florida 32399
850-245-6400
http://www.museumoffloridahistory.com/

Admission Fees: Free, but donations accepted

Hours: Monday-Friday, 9:00 am to 4:30 pm; Saturday 10:00 am
to 4:30 pm; Sunday and holidays, Noon to 4:30 pm

MICANOPY

Micanopy is pronounced Mick A Nopie. It is a small historic village just off US Highway 441 about 20 miles south of Gainesville. The entire town is designated as a National Historic District. The town is named for a famous Seminole chief.

About 700 people live in this town and many of them work in the local antique shops and restaurants. There is also a historic home in town that is currently a bed and breakfast: the Herlong Mansion.

The movie "Doc Hollywood" starring Michael J. Fox and Woody Harrelson was mostly filmed in Micanopy. A great little historic town, McIntosh, is a few miles south of Micanopy.

BASIC INFORMATION

Admission Fees: Free

Hours: 24 hours/day

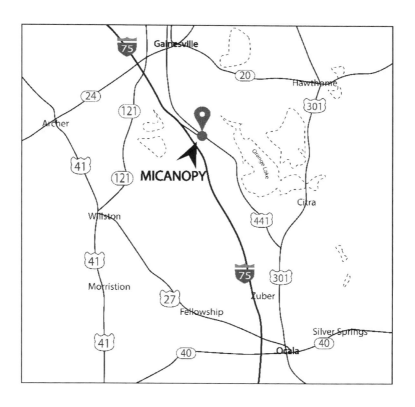

AMELIA ISLAND HORSEBACK RIDING

A woman named Debbie Manser has been operating this unique attraction for more than 25 years. You call her and arrange to meet her and her horses at Peters Point Beachfront Park in Fernandina Beach. She trailers the horses in from their stable close to Amelia Island.

Once you start riding on the beach, you will do so for one hour. Debbie can accommodate two to four riders at one time, but with advanced notice can handle up to six riders. Riding times are flexible in the fall and winter, but only from 11:00 am to 5:00 pm from May 1 until November 1.

You will ride along the beach with either Debbie or one of her guides. You can let your horse amble along in the shallow surf. Like all animals (except maybe cats), they enjoy the soothing sounds and waters of the Atlantic Ocean.

BASIC INFORMATION

Peters Point Road
Amelia Island, Florida 32034
904-753-1701
http://ameliaislandhorsebackriding.com/

Admission Fees: Sunrise or Sunset Rides, $150/person;
Daytime Rides, $100/person

Hours: Varies depending on the season

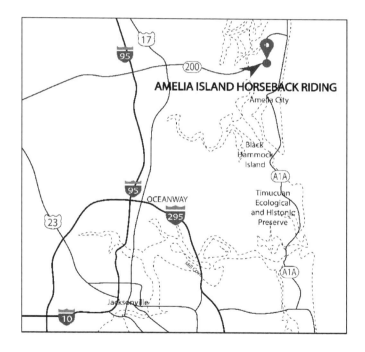

CATTY SHACK RANCH

Catty Shack Ranch is a non-profit wildlife sanctuary in Jacksonville. It has become one of the area's most popular visitor attractions. Their primary mission is to give endangered big cats a permanent home.

They specialize in the rescue of exotic animals who are in danger. When an animal arrives at Catty Shack Ranch, it will have a loving home for the rest of its life. None of these animals is used for breeding, trading, selling, or buying.

Animals currently living at Catty Shack Ranch include tigers, lions, pumas, leopards, lynx, foxes, and coatimundis. Even though the last two aren't cats, they have been given "honorary cat" status by the ranch.

BASIC INFORMATION

1860 Starratt Road
Jacksonville, Florida 32226
904-757-3603
http://cattyshack.org/

Admission Fees: $ 10 Adults, $ 5 children

Hours: Day tours start at 1:00 pm on Thursdays and end at 4:00 pm. Night feeding tours start at 6:00 pm on Fridays, Saturdays, and Wednesdays and end at 8:30 pm. You need to choose your date and tour, then buy tickets online.

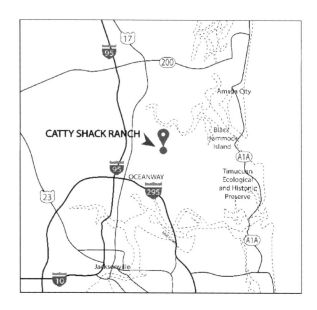

FORT CAROLINE NATIONAL MEMORIAL

Many people don't realize that France and Spain struggled for control of Florida in the sixteenth century. Fort Caroline is on a bluff not far from the mount of the St. Johns River where it meets the Atlantic Ocean. This was France's foothold in the New World.

The exhibits will show you this history, including stories of exploration, survival, religious disputes, territorial battles, and the first contact between Native Americans and Europeans.

The settlement at Fort Caroline did not survive beyond its first year. Spanish troops marched up from St. Augustine and destroyed the settlement and most of its people.

BASIC INFORMATION

12713 Fort Carolina Road
Jacksonville, Florida 32225
904-641-7155
https://www.nps.gov/timu/learn/historyculture/foca.htm

Admission Fees: Free

Hours: 9:00 am to 5:00 pm daily except government holidays

JACKSONVILLE MUSEUM OF SCIENCE AND HISTORY

The Jacksonville Museum of Science and History is located in downtown on the south bank of the St. Johns River. It is a non-profit institution and the city's most visited museum.

The museum was founded in 1941 as the Jacksonville Children's Museum. The current name came about in 1988. Its mission is to increase the knowledge and understanding of the natural environment. It focuses also on the history of Jacksonville and Northeast Florida. Interactive exhibits teach children about the sun, nuclear power, and wind energy.

Permanent and temporary exhibits feature 12,000 years of area history from ancient times through Super Bowl XXXIX. You will see science demonstrations and a popular exhibit, Atlantic Tails, that teaches you about whales, dolphins, and manatees that thrive in the area's waters.

BASIC INFORMATION

1025 Museum Circle
Jacksonville, Florida 32207
904-396-6674
http://themosh.org/

Admission Fees: $12.50 Adults, $ 10 Seniors, Students, Children

Hours: Monday-Thursday 10:00 am to 5:00 pm; Friday 10:00 am to 8:00 pm; Saturday 10:00 am to 6:00 pm; Sunday 12:00 pm to 5:00 pm.

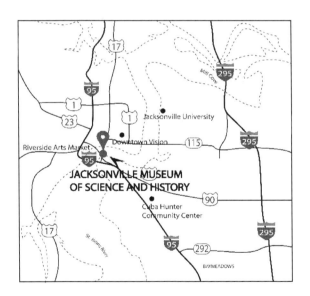

LITTLE TALBOT ISLAND STATE PARK

This state park is north of Jacksonville on one of the few remaining barrier islands on Florida's east coast. You will enjoy nature at its finest, with maritime forests, desert like sand dunes, and pristine salt marshes.

The streams on the west side of the park as well as the Atlantic surf provide great opportunities for fishing. Catches include bluefish, striped bass, redfish, flounder, mullet, and sheepshead.

The park has plenty of places for hiking, kayaking, beachcombing, surfing, and picnics. There is also a campground in the park. Other parks that can be visited from here include Fort George Island Cultural State Park, Amelia Island State Park, and Pumpkin Hill Creek Preserve State Park.

BASIC INFORMATION

12157 Heckscher Drive
Jacksonville, Florida 32226
904-251-2320
https://www.floridastateparks.org/park/Little-Talbot-Island

Admission Fees: $ 5.00/car up to 8 people. Camping extra.

Hours: 8:00 am to Sundown, 365 days/year

MARINELAND

Marineland was one of Florida's earliest attractions and for many years its most popular. It was founded in 1938 as Marine Studios, and was known as the "World's First Oceanarium". It was the pre-eminent institution for breeding and researching bottlenose dolphins.

The Marineland of today has a mission of fostering the preservation of marine life and to use interactive education and onsite research to inspire visitors to value and respect marine mammals and their environment.

This is an attraction where you can touch and feed dolphins, have a birthday party for your kids or friends, and experience a dolphin adventure where you get into the water with the friendly animals.

BASIC INFORMATION

9600 Oceanshore Boulevard
St. Augustine, Florida 32080
904-471-1111
http://www.marineland.net/

Admission Fees: There are a variety of adventures with different fees. $36.95 gives you a touch and feed experience; up to $485 dollars to work with a trainer for a day.

Hours: Hours may vary, but are generally 9:00 am to 4:30 pm.

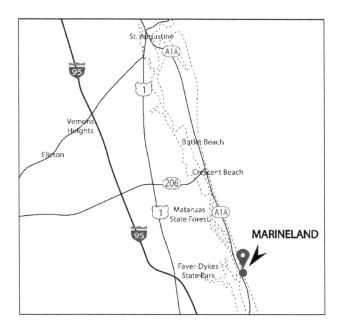

ST AUGUSTINE CASTILLO SAN MARCOS

This ancient fort is the centerpiece of downtown St. Augustine. A favorite way to enjoy this attraction is to take yourself and family on a self guided tour. Maps are provided and you go into and out of the various rooms and experience what conditions must have been like in the old days.

The structure was built between 1672-1695 by the Spanish to guard the approach to the waters of St. Augustine. The fort was built using local coquina rock, which is a limestone consisting almost entirely of sea shells and fossils.

In addition to Spain, other flags have flown over the Castillo in its long history, including Britain and the United States of America.

BASIC INFORMATION

1 South Castillo Drive
St. Augustine, Florida 32084
904-829-6506
https://www.nps.gov/casa/index.htm

Admission Fees: $ 10.00 adults, children under 15 free

Hours: 8:45 am to 5:00 pm every day except Thanksgiving and
Christmas

SAN SEBASTIAN WINERY

This family owned winery has been in business since 1996 and has become a favorite St. Augustine attraction. It is the second largest winery in Florida, and over 160,000 visitors a year come in to taste wine and tour the facility.

There is a gourmet gift shop, and the facility has 18,000 square feet with storage capacity of 40,000 gallons of wine. You can purchase appetizers and wines, as well as domestic and imported beers. Native varieties of red Noble, bronze Carlos and Welder Muscadines are grown for the winery by Lakeridge Winery Estate and Prosperity Vineyards.

There is an open air deck where you can enjoy your wine and snacks while listening to music. The view of St. Augustine is wonderful from the deck, and the music is provided every Friday, Saturday, and Sunday.

BASIC INFORMATION

157 King Street
St. Augustine, Florida 32084
904-826-1594
http://www.sansebastianwinery.com

Admission Fees: Free

Hours: Monday-Saturday 10:00 am to 6:00 pm: Sunday 11:00
am to 6:00 pm.

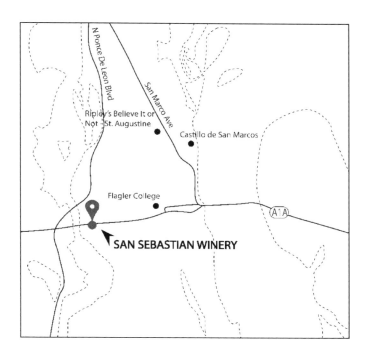

FORT LAUDERDALE WATER TAXI

The water taxi is an enjoyable way to visit and explore the Fort Lauderdale area. They have a fleet of 14 vessels, some of them with on board amenities. You can enjoy your trip as an individual, family, or even as a group with a special reservation.

As you cruise along the waterways your captain will point out mansions of famous people, landmarks, and fill you in on the history of the area you are visiting. You will see hundreds of mega yachts because this is the yachting capital of the world.

You can board a vessel at any one of 15 different locations and ride the taxi all day. Their website has a map showing you where these locations are. Your ticket gives you the right to get on or off at any of these locations for a one day period. You can also buy monthly or annual passes.

It is good manners to leave your crew members a tip.

BASIC INFORMATION

Any of several locations from north of Oakland Park Blvd south to Hollywood Beach and west to Esplanade Park on the New River. See the map on their website for boarding locations. 954-467-6677

http://watertaxi.com/

Admission Fees: $28.00 Adult all day (12-64); $18.00 Happy Hour (5:00 pm to Close); Special Senior and children rates.

Hours: Sunday-Thursday: 10:00 am to 10:00 pm, Fridays and Saturdays: 10:00 am to 11:00 pm

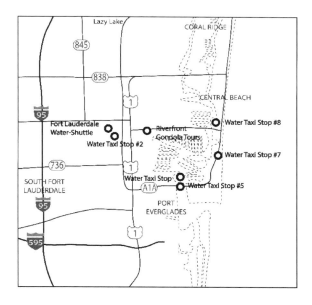

GUMBO LIMBO NATURE CENTER

Gumbo Limbo Nature Center was founded in 1984. More than 200,000 visitors last year enjoyed the boardwalk, tropical fish in the aquariums, and the butterfly garden. They also enjoy looking at the sea turtle rehabilitation facility.

This center is devoted to environmental education, research, and conservation. It is 20 acres in size and is located on the barrier island between the Intracoastal Waterway and the Atlantic Ocean.

Many of the endangered plants and animals on the barrier island seek refuge in this lush environment. Visitors enjoy a nature walk along the quarter mile long boardwalk through a preserved hardwood hammock. You will see gumbo limbo, strangler fig, cabbage palm, and animals like foxes and skinks.

BASIC INFORMATION

1801 North Ocean Boulevard
Boca Raton, Florida 33432
561-544-8605
https://www.gumbolimbo.org/

Admission Fees: Free, but $5.00 donation is welcome.

Hours: Nature Center & Aquarium: Mon-Sat 9:00 am 4:00 pm;
Sunday 12:00 pm – 4:00 pm. Nature Trails: Mon-Sat 7am-dusk

JUPITER INLET LIGHTHOUSE

Jupiter Inlet Lighthouse & Museum is a wonderful place to visit and learn about the history of this part of Florida. The museum contains artifacts and displays covering 5,000 years of history. Native American culture is shown, along with information about the first settlers in the Jupiter area.

The lighthouse and museum are operated by the Loxahatchee River History Society. For many people, the highlight of their visit is the walk up to the top of the lighthouse. It is a strenuous climb and recommended only for people with no health problems.

The view from the top of the lighthouse is spectacular. You can see north along Jupiter Island all the way to the south and buildings in Palm Beach County. Jupiter Inlet itself is a thing of beauty and one of Florida's most popular ocean inlets.

BASIC INFORMATION

500 Captain Armour's Way
Jupiter, Florida 33469
561-747-8380
https://www.jupiterlighthouse.org/

Admission Fees: $12 adults, $6 children

Hours: 7 days/week 10:00 am to 5:00 pm (January through April 29). Tuesday-Sunday 10:00 am to 5:00 pm (May through December

LION COUNTRY SAFARI

Lion Country Safari is an unusual amusement park that allows you to drive your own car through their grounds. You can spend an entire day driving among their more than 1,000 animals.

The attraction also has rides and a water spray feature for the kids, animal feeding experiences, restaurant, shops, a campground, and a lot more. It's a theme park with a more reasonable cost than the big ones in Orlando.

Some of the animals you will see include tortoises, tapirs, alpaca, impala, ostrich, water buffalo, lion, ankole cattle, rhinoceros, zebra, chimpanzee, and thousands more.

There is a sister attraction, Safari World, that costs less and lets you walk through the animal exhibits.

BASIC INFORMATION

2003 Lion Country Safari Road
Loxahatchee, Florida 33470
561-793-1084
http://www.lioncountrysafari.com/

Admission Fees: $35 Adult (10-64); $26 children. Parking $8

Hours: Open every day from 9:30 am to 4:30 pm

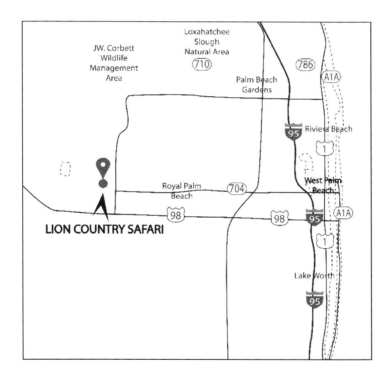

MIAMI SEAQUARIUM

Miami Seaquarium is located on Virginia Key between downtown Miami and Key Biscayne. It is along the Rickenbacker Causeway, and has a spectacular view of both the Miami and Key Biscayne skylines.

The 38 acre attraction has many child friendly experiences and the entire family will enjoy a visit. You can see and interact with dolphins, sea lions, sting rays, sharks, birds, fish and more. There are shows where you can see dolphins and sea lions perform. The shows are both entertaining and educational. You will learn about each mammal's lifestyle.

The focus at Miami Seaquarium is on education and conservation, and they have many interactive programs and exhibits. This is one of the few places in Florida where you can swim with the dolphins and have other encounters. You can even find yourself in an environment with penguins.

BASIC INFORMATION

4400 Rickenbacker Causeway
Miami, Florida 33149
305-361-5705
https://www.miamiseaquarium.com/

Admission Fees: $45.99 (Age 10+); $35.99 (Age 3-9)

Hours: 7 days/week, 10:00 am to 6:00 pm. Subject to change without notice so call before going.

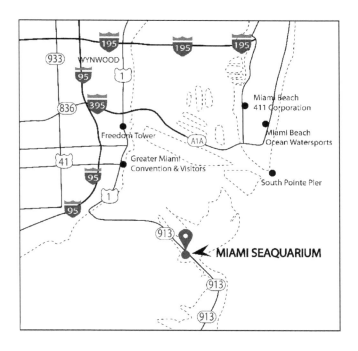

MORIKAMI GARDENS

Morikami Museum and Japanese Gardens has Japanese cultural exhibits that educate and inspire visitors. The history of this attraction has its roots in Yamato Colony, a small community of Japanese pioneers in 1904 near Boca Raton and Delray Beach.

The museum building is modeled after a Japanese villa, and has exhibition rooms surrounding an open courtyard with a dry garden of gravel, pebbles, and small boulders. The building also has a 225 seat theater and an authentic tea house and a café.

The 16 acre grounds around the museum include Japanese gardens with walking paths, rest areas, and a large bonsai collection. The entire park contains 200 acres and has nature trails, pine forests, and picnic areas.

BASIC INFORMATION

4000 Morikami Park Road
Delray Beach, Florida 33446
561-495-0233
https://morikami.org/

Admission Fees: $15 Adults, $9 Children 6-17

Hours: Tuesday-Sunday: 10:00 am to 5:00 pm; Closed
Mondays and Major Holidays

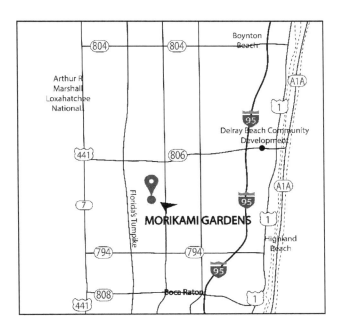

THEATER OF THE SEA

Theater of the Sea is a family owned venture and has been in business since 1946. It is one of the oldest marine facilities in the world. The lagoons and tropical gardens are home to dolphins, sea lions, sea turtles, tropical fish, game fish, sharks, stingrays, alligators, birds, and others.

You will get to observe various shows from a close distance involving dolphins, sea lions, parrots, and other animals. There are also many interactive programs such as swimming with a sea lion or a dolphin. You can get up close to sea turtles and even alligators.

Attractions include a bottomless boat ride, a fish and reptile tour, walking on a lagoon beach, and much more. The dolphin swims are 30 minutes and include dorsal tows, kisses and hugs, and swimming and snorkeling with a dolphin.

BASIC INFORMATION

84721 Overseas Highway
Mile Marker 84.5
Islamorada, Florida 33036
https://theaterofthesea.com/

Admission Fees: Adults $35.95, Children (3-10) $22.95

Hours: Open every day from 9:30 am to 3:30 pm

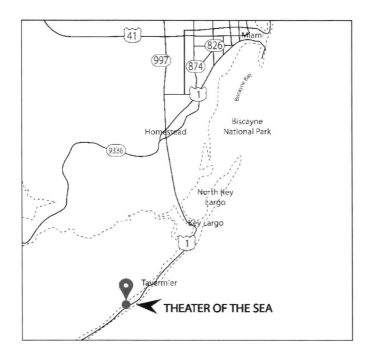

THE DOLPHIN CONNECTION

The Dolphin Connection has been in business since 1990 and is located at the Hawks Cay Resort and Marina. As the name implies, they focus on dolphins and have a world-wide reputation as experts on the bottlenose dolphin.

The facility is centered around a circular salt water lagoon. You will be able to meet dolphins face to face and will be amazed at the obvious intelligence and natural good nature of these friendly mammals. The owners and employees of this facility believe in providing the highest possible care to their dolphins.

There are various levels of dolphin experiences available from **Dockside Dolphins** (30 minutes, 15 minutes with dolphins, **Dolphin Discovery** (45 minutes, 25 minutes with dolphins), and **Trainer for a Day** (3 hours).

BASIC INFORMATION

61 Hawks Cay Boulevard
Duck Key, Florida 33050
305-289-0136
https://www.dolphinconnection.com

Admission Fees: Programs from $69 to $329 per person

Hours: Open every day from 9:00 am to 5:00 pm

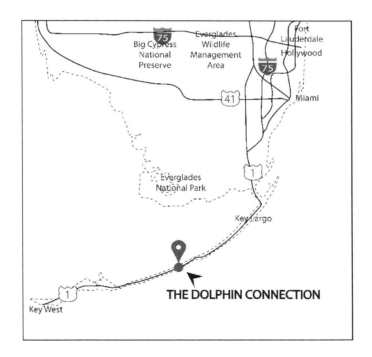

Made in the USA
Columbia, SC
09 April 2019